On Four Wheels

John Allan

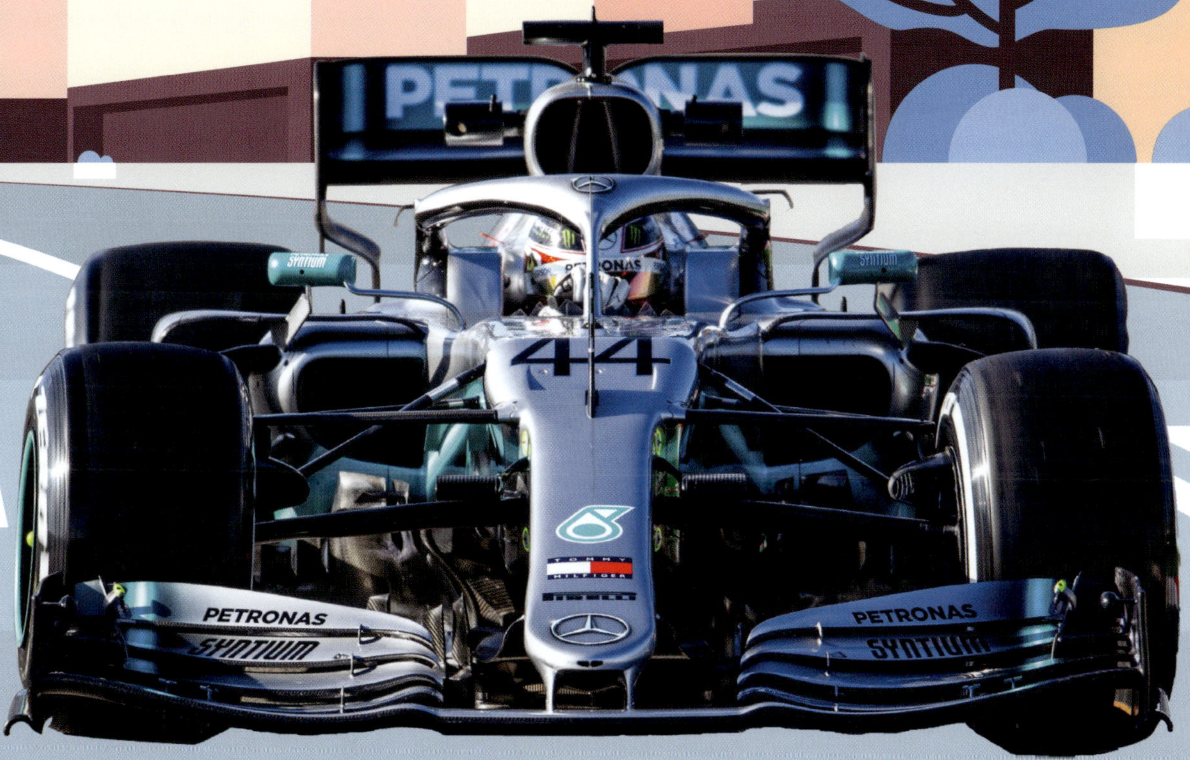

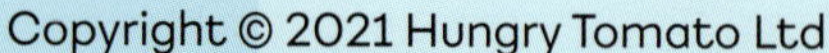

Copyright © 2021 Hungry Tomato Ltd

First published in Great Britain in 2021 by
Hungry Tomato Ltd
F1, Old Bakery Studios
Blewetts Wharf
Malpas Road, Truro
Cornwall, TR1 1QH, UK

No part of this publications may be reproduced, stored in a retrieval system, or transmitted in any form or by any means, electronic, mechanical, photocopying, recording, or otherwise, without the prior written permission of the copyright owner.

A CIP catalog record for this book is available from the British Library

ISBN 978 1 913440 61 9

Manufactured in the USA

Discover more at
www.hungrytomato.com

Contents

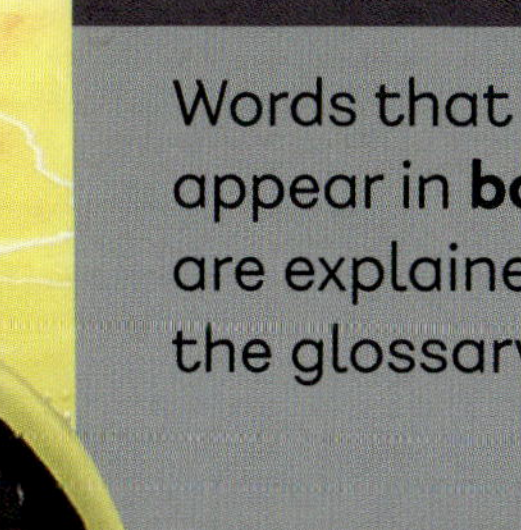

Words that appear in **bold** are explained in the glossary

The Mighty Mechanics

We are the **Mighty Mechanics.** Welcome to our **workshop**. We work on some amazing vehicles, and here are a few of the **tools** we use to fix them.

A wrench is used to loosen large bolts.

A good mechanic always has a tidy toolbox to keep their tools in.

Bugatti Chiron

This is the **fastest car in the world**. It has reached speeds of over 305 mph (49 km/h).

This Bugatti is so powerful it needs ten **radiators** to keep the engine cool.

This is an early Type 35 Bugatti.

This **hypercar** is very expensive! It costs $2.5 million!

The Chiron can go from 0-60 mph (97km/h) in just 2.3 seconds!

Truck Racing

Trucks are often called 'Kings of the Road'. Now, trucks are found on race tracks as well, and can speed around them at 100 mph (161 km/h).

The driver is protected by a **roll cage.**

This truck is competing in the Baja 1000, a non-stop, off-road race.
The brakes are water-cooled so that they don't overheat.
These mighty machines weigh 6 tons (12,000 pounds).
RENAULT
TRUCKS
RACING
TOTAL

Formula 1

This is the most popular motorsport in the world, with nearly 2 billion people watching the races each year.

The steering wheel has 20 different buttons to use while racing.

It takes this many mechanics to change tires during a race.

The **aerodynamics** on these cars is so powerful that they could drive across a ceiling without falling off.

Formula 1 cars can go from 0 to 100 mph (161 km/h) and back again in under 4 seconds.

Koenigsegg Agera

This **supercar** is one of the top 5 fastest cars on the planet, with a top speed of 278 mph (447 km/h).

This car cost a cool $2.5 million and only 25 were built.

The Agera has a removable roof.

The doors on this car lift out and up by just pressing a button!

The world's most expensive car key belongs to an Agera. It costs $250,000 and contains diamonds!

Thrust SSC

This was the first car to break the **sound barrier** when it reached a speed of 763 mph (1,228 km/h). SSC stands for supersonic car.

It is powered by two jet engines.

British Royal Airforce pilot Andy Green set the current **land speed record** in the Thrust SSC in 1997.

The SSC Bloodhound will be the next car to try and break the 1,000 mph (1609 km/h) barrier.

It took just 16 seconds for Thrust SCC to go from 0 to 600 mph (1,000 km/h).

Shockwave Truck

This superfast truck has three **jet engines** in the back to push it along at 376 mph (605 km/h).

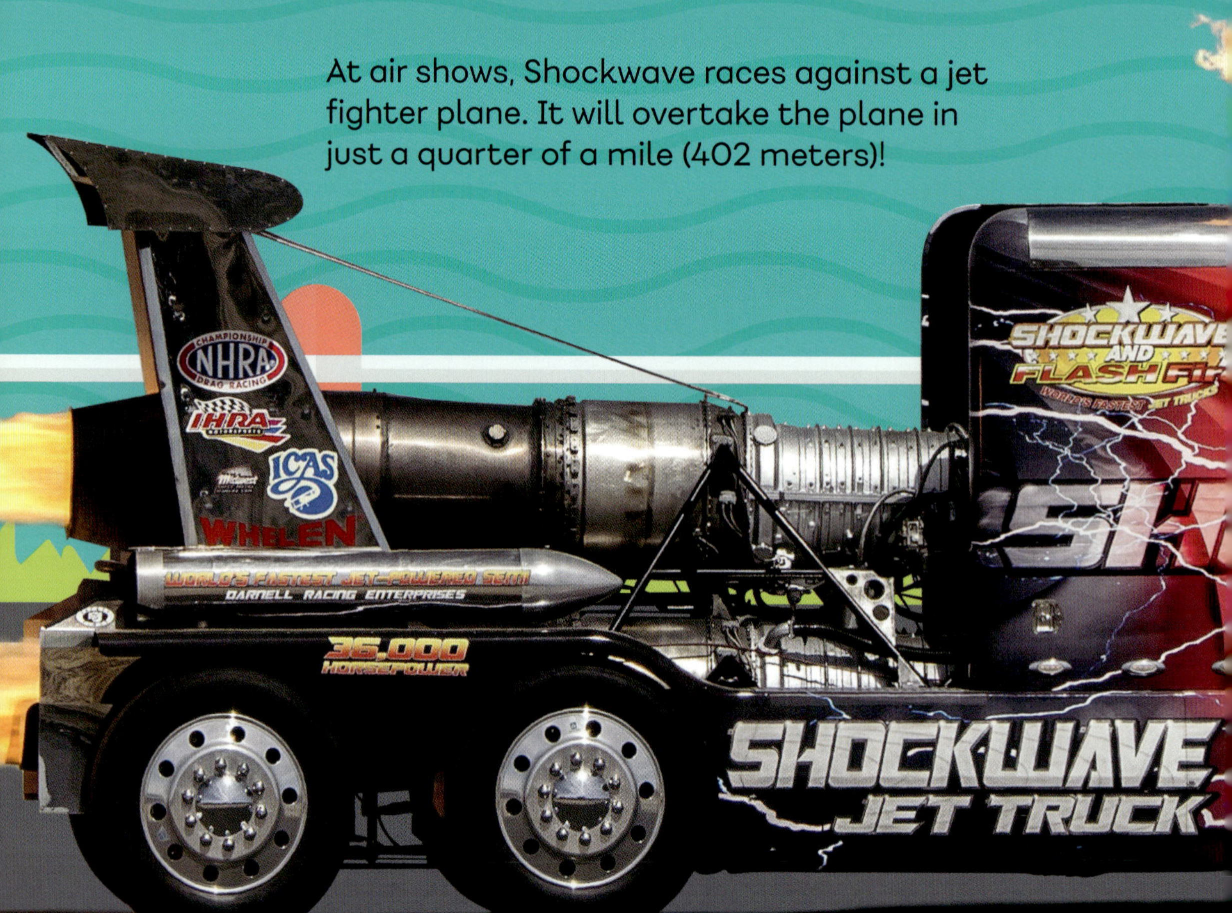

At air shows, Shockwave races against a jet fighter plane. It will overtake the plane in just a quarter of a mile (402 meters)!

Shockwave burns through 180 gallons (810 liters) of jet fuel each time it races.

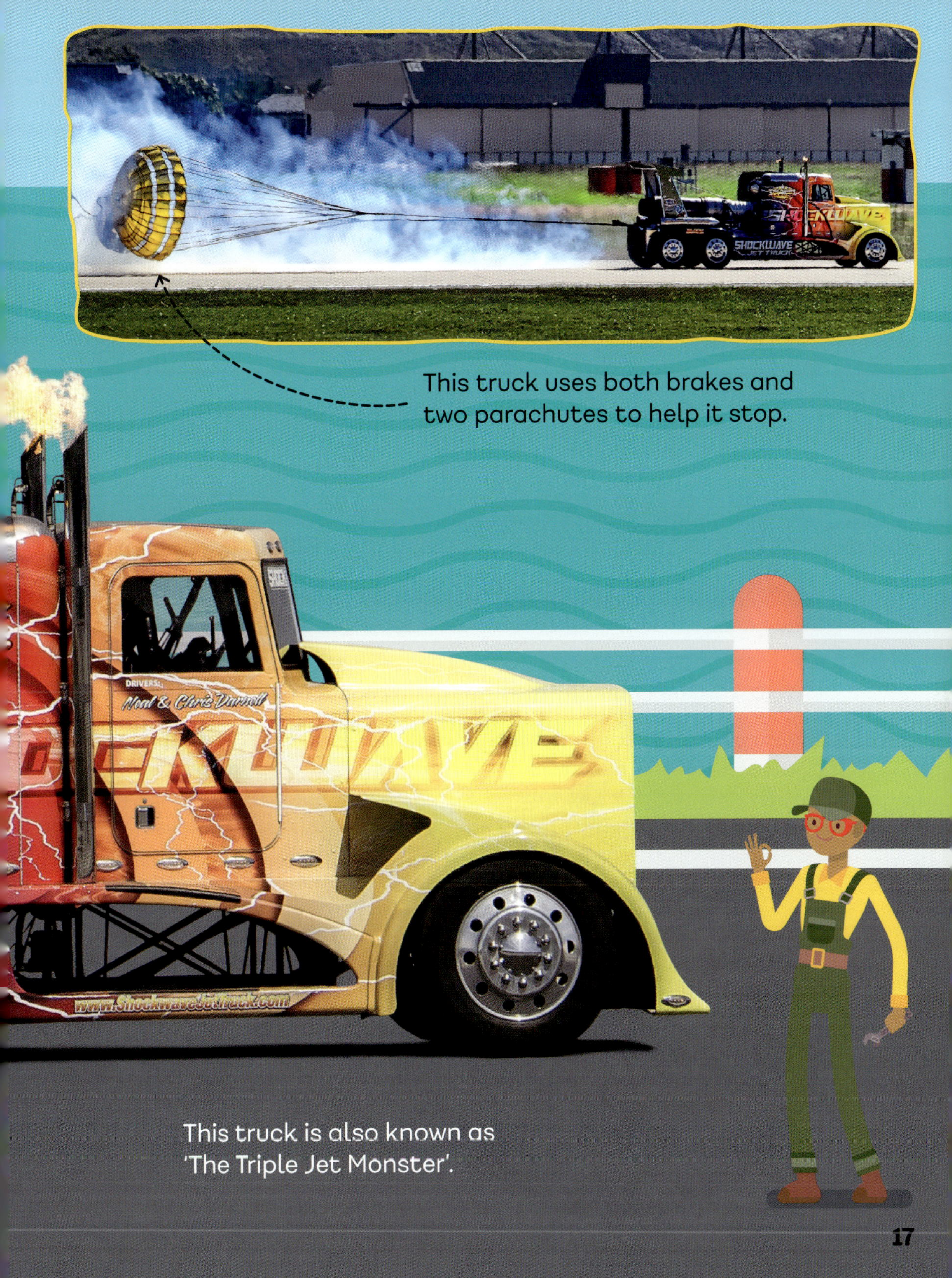

This truck uses both brakes and two parachutes to help it stop.

This truck is also known as 'The Triple Jet Monster'.

Ford F-150 Raptor

This truck is built to perform, both on and off the road. On the road, it can reach 60 mph (96.5 km/h) in just over 6 seconds.

The Ford Raptor is designed to tackle extreme conditions off road, including desert sand and fresh snow.

This truck has a supersized 5.5 liter V6 engine.

This Ford is named after a family of strong, sharp-eyed birds, called raptors.

Ford F-series trucks have been made since the 1940s.

Funny Cars Drag Racing

Drag racing is a test of how fast a car can go in a quarter of a mile. These cars have short bodies and large wheels at the back.

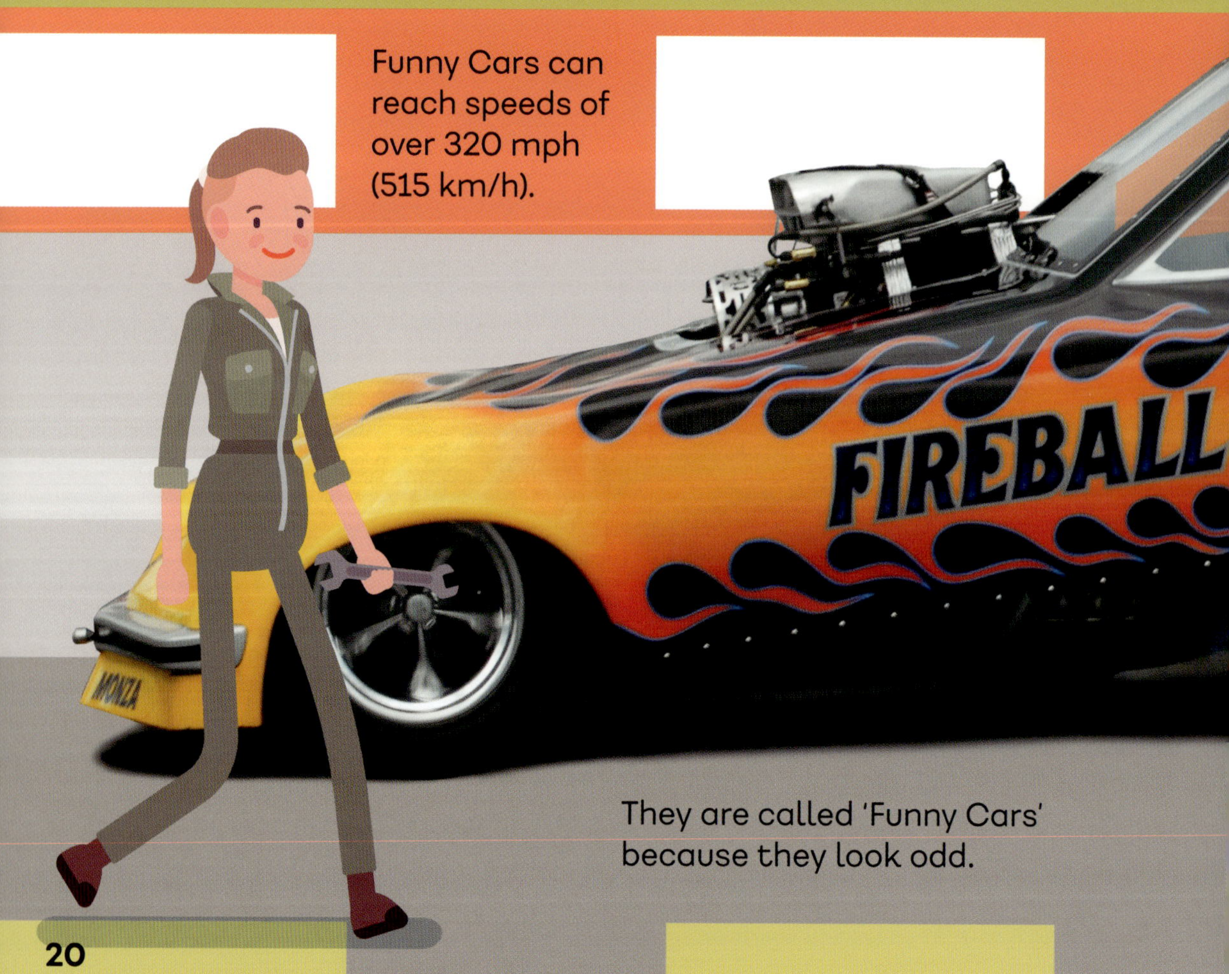

Funny Cars can reach speeds of over 320 mph (515 km/h).

They are called 'Funny Cars' because they look odd.

These cars go so fast that they need parachutes to help them stop.

These superfast cars use the same type of fuel as jet planes.

Monster Truck

These massive trucks race and perform tricks in big arenas packed with **spectators**.

Their supercharged engines have twice the power of a formula 1 race car.

These trucks have a top speed of 100 mph (162 km/h).

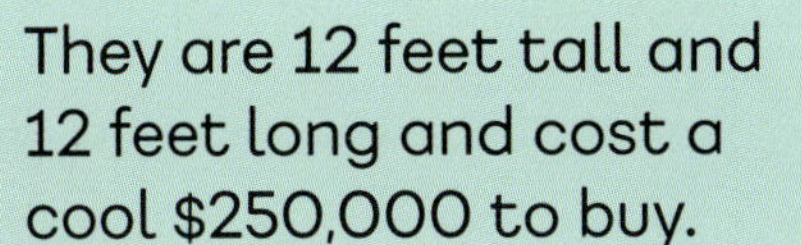

They are 12 feet tall and 12 feet long and cost a cool $250,000 to buy.

Monster trucks can jump, crash and perform amazing stunts.

Glossary

aerodynamics is how air moves over an object. So, the more aerodynamic a car is the faster it will go.

hypercar top sports cars are called supercars. The best and most powerful supercars are known as hypercars.

land speed record is the record for the highest speed reached by a person using a vehicle on land.

radiators remove heat from a car to stop it overheating.

roll cage is a frame that is built around a driver's seat to protect them if they crash.

sound barrier is the speed that sound travels at.

spectators are people watching a show or event.

Measuring Speed

A vehicle's speed is usually measured in either **miles per hour (mph)** or **kilometers per hour (km/h).**

1 mph = 1.6 km/h

Picture Credits

(abbreviations: t = top; b = bottom; m = middle; l = left; r = right; bg = background)

Shutterstock: Andrew Rybalko (mechanics illustrations); Andrey Armyagov 5ml; Angyalosi Beata 15t; BoJack 18m; Bruce Alan Bennett 20m; BW Press 22m, 23tr; CHEN WS 11tl; ClickyClarkPhotos 7tr; dimcars 13tr; DniproDD 2bg; Ev. Safronov 1m, 10m; EvrenKalinbacak 8m; Grindstone Media Group 21tr; Julia Lazebnaya 9bg, 18bg; Knumina Studios 17t; Maksim Toome 6m; Maksim Vivtsaruk 4mr; Mastak A 16bg, 24bg; matrioshka 20bg; MicroOne 6bg; Oleksandr Derevianko 14bg, 22bg; Ondrej Prosicky 19tr; patruflo 14m; ProStockStudio 1bg, 10bg, 12bg; Rodrigo Garrido 9tr; Santiparp Wattanaporn 16m; Sebastian D92 12m; TheFarAwayKingdom 4ml; Vectorpocket 4bg.

Every effort has been made to trace the copyright holders and we apologise in advance for any unintentional omissions. We would be pleased to insert the appropriate acknowledgement in any subsequent edition of this publication